NPL F
Nashville Public Library | FOUNDATION

This book given
to the Nashville Public Library
through the generosity of the
Dollar General
Literacy Foundation

NUMBERS 1–20

Know Your Numbers

TOYS

Mary Elizabeth Salzmann

Consulting Editor, Diane Craig, M.A./Reading Specialist

Sandcastle

An Imprint of Abdo Publishing
www.abdopublishing.com

visit us at www.abdopublishing.com

Published by Abdo Publishing, a division of ABDO, PO Box 398166, Minneapolis, Minnesota 55439. Copyright © 2015 by Abdo Consulting Group, Inc. International copyrights reserved in all countries. No part of this book may be reproduced in any form without written permission from the publisher. SandCastle™ is a trademark and logo of Abdo Publishing.

Printed in the United States of America, North Mankato, Minnesota
062014
092014

THIS BOOK CONTAINS
RECYCLED MATERIALS

Editor: Alex Kuskowski
Content Developer: Nancy Tuminelly
Cover and Interior Design: Anders Hanson, Mighty Media, Inc.
Photo Credits: Shutterstock

Library of Congress Cataloging-in-Publication Data
Salzmann, Mary Elizabeth, 1968- author.
  Know your numbers. Toys / Mary Elizabeth Salzmann.
      pages cm. -- (Numbers 1-20)
  Audience: Ages 3-9.
  ISBN 978-1-62403-269-1
1. Counting--Juvenile literature. 2. Cardinal numbers--Juvenile literature. 3. Toys--Juvenile literature. I. Title. II. Title:
Toys.
  QA113.S295 2015
  513.2--dc23
                          2013041918

SandCastle™ Level: Beginning

SandCastle™ books are created by a team of professional educators, reading specialists, and content developers around five essential components—phonemic awareness, phonics, vocabulary, text comprehension, and fluency—to assist young readers as they develop reading skills and strategies and increase their general knowledge. All books are written, reviewed, and leveled for guided reading, early reading intervention, and Accelerated Reader® programs for use in shared, guided, and independent reading and writing activities to support a balanced approach to literacy instruction. The SandCastle™ series has four levels that correspond to early literacy development. The levels are provided to help teachers and parents select appropriate books for young readers.

EMERGING · **BEGINNING** · TRANSITIONAL · FLUENT

Contents

There is 1 fire truck.
It has a ladder on top.

• = 1 = one

1 2 3 4 5 6 7 8 9 10 11 12 13 14 15 16 17 18 19 20

There are 2 game controllers.
Amanda plays with her Aunt Meg.

●● = 2 = two

1 2 3 4 5 6 7 8 9 10 11 12 13 14 15 16 17 18 19 20

Andrea has 3 beach balls.
She shares with Lily and Jenna.

••• = 3 = three

Kayla peeks into her dollhouse.
There are 4 chairs at the table.

●●●● = 4 = four

1 2 3 **4** 5 6 7 8 9 10 11 12 13 14 15 16 17 18 19 20

Alexis draws on the blackboard.
She draws 5 hearts.

There are 6 stuffed animals.
They are shaped like bunnies.

●●●●● = 6 = six

1 2 3 4 5 6 7 8 9 10 11 12 13 14 15 16 17 18 19 20

There are 7 rubber ducks.
They are fun to play with in the bath.

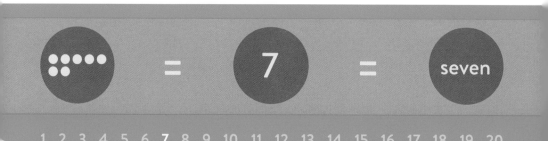

●●●●● = 7 = seven

1 2 3 4 5 6 **7** 8 9 10 11 12 13 14 15 16 17 18 19 20

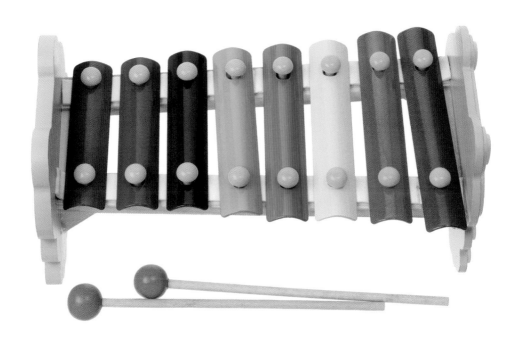

The **xylophone** has 8 keys.
Each key makes a different sound.

1 2 3 4 5 6 7 **8** 9 10 11 12 13 14 15 16 17 18 19 20

There are 9 instruments.
They make loud music.

⚫⚫⚫⚫⚫
⚫⚫⚫⚫ = 9 = nine

1 2 3 4 5 6 7 8 **9** 10 11 12 13 14 15 16 17 18 19 20

Paige has 10 finger **puppets**.
There is a puppet on each finger.

| ●●●●● ●●●●● | = | 10 | = | ten |

1 2 3 4 5 6 7 8 9 **10** 11 12 13 14 15 16 17 18 19 20

There are 11 robots.
Most of them have square heads.

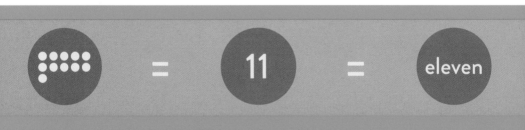

= 11 = eleven

1 2 3 4 5 6 7 8 9 10 **11** 12 13 14 15 16 17 18 19 20

Checkers has red and black pieces.
There are 12 of each color.

Sam is playing a card game.
He has 13 cards in his hand.

= 13 = thirteen

1 2 3 4 5 6 7 8 9 10 11 12 **13** 14 15 16 17 18 19 20

It's Evan's birthday! He has
14 balloons at his birthday party.

⬤⬤⬤⬤⬤ = 14 = fourteen

1 2 3 4 5 6 7 8 9 10 11 12 13 **14** 15 16 17 18 19 20

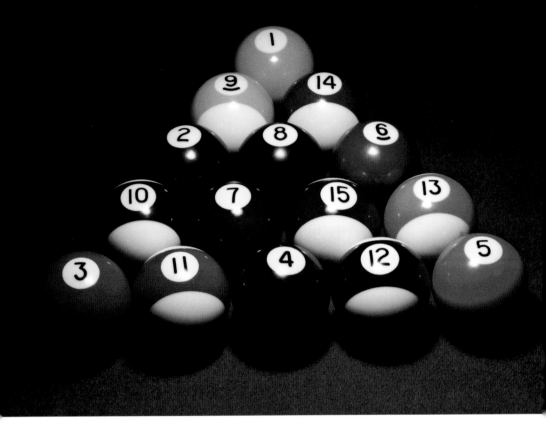

There are 15 pool balls.
Some are solid. Some are striped.

The jacks are on the red **tablecloth**.
There are 16 jacks.

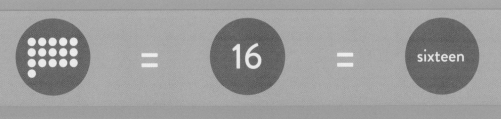

$$\vcenter{\hbox{⣿⣿}} = 16 = \text{sixteen}$$

1 2 3 4 5 6 7 8 9 10 11 12 13 14 15 **16** 17 18 19 20

Abby likes to blow bubbles.
She can blow 17 bubbles at once!

= 17 = seventeen

1 2 3 4 5 6 7 8 9 10 11 12 13 14 15 16 **17** 18 19 20

There are 18 cars. They are red,
blue, green, and yellow.

= 18 = eighteen

1 2 3 4 5 6 7 8 9 10 11 12 13 14 15 16 17 **18** 19 20

Micah plays with **pick-up sticks.**
There are 19 sticks.

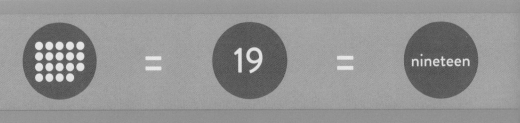

= 19 = nineteen

1 2 3 4 5 6 7 8 9 10 11 12 13 14 15 16 17 18 **19** 20

There are 20 blocks. The blocks
have a different color on each side.

= 20 = twenty

Glossary

pick-up sticks – a game in which the players try pick up one stick from a pile of sticks, without moving the other sticks.

xylophone – an instrument played by tapping keys with a mallet.

puppet – a doll that can be moved by strings, a stick, or a hand placed inside it.

tablecloth – a cloth that covers the top of a table.